Jackie Robinson

by Morgan Lloyd

Editorial Offices: Glenview, Illinois • Needham, Massachusetts • New York, New York
Sales Offices: Needham, Massachusetts • Duluth, Georgia • Glenview, Illinois
Coppell, Texas • Ontario, California • Mesa, Arizona

Every effort has been made to secure permission and provide appropriate credit for photographic material. The publisher deeply regrets any omission and pledges to correct errors called to its attention in subsequent editions.

Unless otherwise acknowledged, all photographs are the property of Scott Foresman, a division of Pearson Education.

Photo locators denoted as follows: Top (T), Center (C), Bottom (B), Left (L), Right (R), Background (Bkgd)

Cover ©Bettmann/Corbis; 1 ©Bettmann/Corbis; 4 (BL) ©Lake County Museum/Corbis, 4 (BR) ©Bettmann/Corbis; 6 ©Hulton Archive/Getty Images; 8 ©Bettmann/Corbis; 9 ©Bettmann/Corbis; 10 ©Sporting News/Sporting News/Getty Images; p11 ©Sporting News/Sporting News/Getty Images; 13 ©Bettmann/Corbis; 14 ©Bettmann/Corbis; 15 ©Bettmann/Corbis; 17 ©Bettmann/Corbis; 18-19 ©Bettmann/Corbis; 20 ©Bettmann/Corbis; p21 ©Bettmann/Corbis; 22 ©Bettmann/Corbis; 23 (TR) ©Bettmann/Corbis, 23 (TL) ©Bettmann/Corbis, 23 (BR) ©Bettmann/Corbis

ISBN: 0-328-13411-2

Copyright © Pearson Education, Inc.

All Rights Reserved. Printed in the United States of America. This publication is protected by Copyright, and permission should be obtained from the publisher prior to any prohibited reproduction, storage in a retrieval system, or transmission in any form by any means, electronic, mechanical, photocopying, recording, or likewise. For information regarding permission(s), write to: Permissions Department, Scott Foresman, 1900 East Lake Avenue, Glenview, Illinois 60025.

5 6 7 8 9 10 V0G1 14 13 12 11 10 09 08 07

CONTENTS

Introduction	4
The Early Years	6
Beginnings in Baseball	11
The Major Leagues	15
Jackie's Legacy	19
Now Try This	22

Introduction

On April 15, 1947, Jackie Robinson stepped out of the dugout at Ebbets Field in Brooklyn, New York. The number 42 was displayed proudly on his blue-and-white jersey as he crossed the field to take his place at first base.

It was Opening Day for the Brooklyn Dodgers, and Jackie Robinson was about to make history. For more than half a century, no African American player had played in the Major Leagues. An invisible "color barrier" had kept talented African American players out of organized baseball.

Until 1947, professional baseball was **segregated**. Only white players could play Major League baseball, where they had contracts, regular schedules, and earned enough money to make a living.

African American players were restricted to the Negro Leagues or foreign leagues in Mexico and Latin America. Playing in these leagues, they earned far less and had harder schedules. Negro League teams had a hard time traveling too. In the South, racist laws known as Jim Crow laws kept many hotels and restaurants open to "whites only." So African American players often went without meals or slept on their busses.

There were more than two dozen teams in the Negro Leagues, and there were hundreds of talented players. But they were not allowed to play in the Majors. Jackie Robinson changed all that. But it wasn't easy.

The Early Years

Jack Roosevelt Robinson was born January 31, 1919, in Cairo, Georgia. Jackie had four older siblings: Edgar, Frank, Mack, and Willa Mae. His father was a **sharecropper** for a white landowner in Cairo, working hard on the land for little pay. Jackie's father grew tired of this way of life, and when Jackie was only one year old, his father left the family in search of better work. He never returned, though, so Mallie, Jackie's mother, was left alone with the five children.

The Robinson Family. Jackie is second from left.

In 1920, when Jackie was just sixteen months old, his mother packed up the family and took a train to Pasadena, California, where her brother lived. Mallie soon found work doing laundry and housekeeping. At first, the family lived with Mallie's brother, but as soon as they could, the family moved into a house on Pepper Street, in a neighborhood that was entirely white.

Since Jackie's mother had to work so hard to support the family, there was no one home to take care of Jackie. During the day, he would go to school with his sister Willa Mae. As he was still too young for school, Jackie spent the day outside in the sandbox, playing by himself. Even with his mother working as hard as she could, there was often not enough money for food. Sometimes Mallie brought food home from the wealthy houses where she worked.

As a child, Jackie liked all kinds of sports and games, and he loved to win. When he was old enough to go to school, he quickly realized that he was an excellent soccer player. All of the other kids wanted Jackie on their team and would give him extra snacks to get him to play on their side.

In high school and junior college, Jackie continued to shine in sports, receiving many offers of **scholarships** from major colleges. Because he wanted to stay close to his mother and help support her, Jackie decided to go to the University of California at Los Angeles (UCLA).

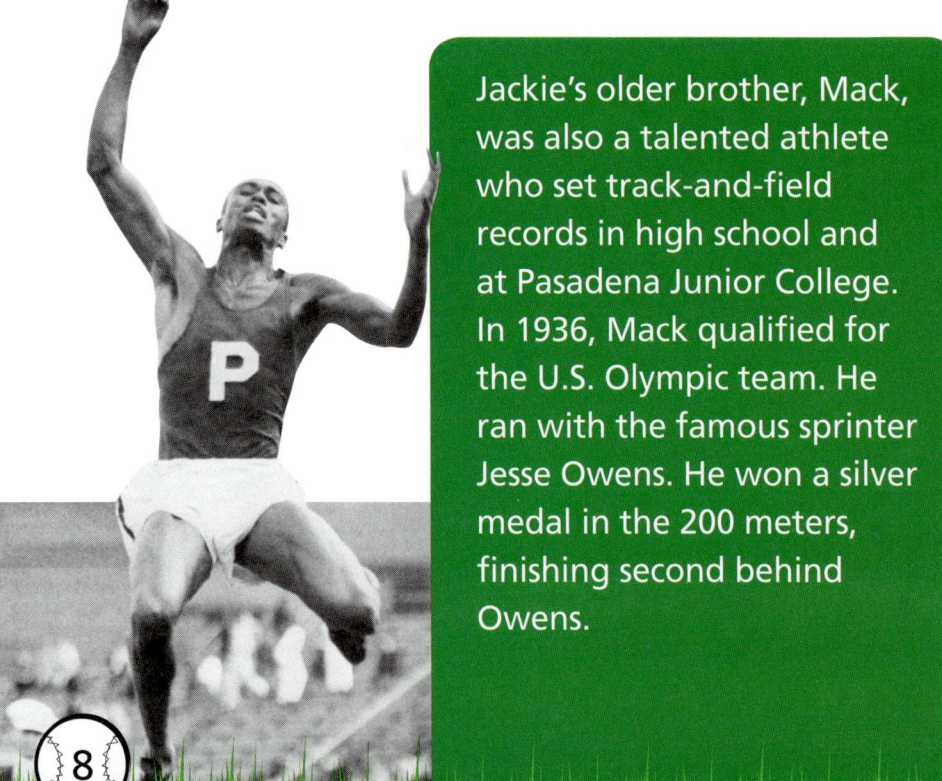

Jackie's older brother, Mack, was also a talented athlete who set track-and-field records in high school and at Pasadena Junior College. In 1936, Mack qualified for the U.S. Olympic team. He ran with the famous sprinter Jesse Owens. He won a silver medal in the 200 meters, finishing second behind Owens.

Jackie was an all-around athlete, excelling in many sports.

At UCLA, Jackie competed in more than half a dozen sports and reached new levels of athletic achievement. Jackie was the leading scorer in basketball; he won a golf championship; and he made it to the semifinals of the National Negro Tennis Tournament. He also won several swimming championships, ran track, and played baseball. But by far, his favorite sport was football. With Jackie on the team, UCLA was undefeated in 1939.

Perhaps the most important thing that happened to Jackie while he was at UCLA is that he met Rachel Isum. Rachel and Jackie became close friends, and in 1942, they became engaged. Jackie did not graduate from UCLA. He was anxious to earn money to support his mother, and he felt that because he was African American, even a college degree would not guarantee him a good job.

Not long after he left UCLA, Pearl Harbor was attacked, and the United States entered World War II. Jackie was drafted and served two years in the army. Since he had an injury to his ankle from football, Jackie was never sent into combat.

Beginnings in Baseball

When he left the army in 1944, Jackie was twenty-five years old. A friend he had met in the army told him that the Kansas City Monarchs (a Negro team) were looking for players. Jackie wrote a letter to the coach and was invited to the spring tryouts.

Soon after the tryouts, Jackie signed a contract for the 1945 season. Though he loved playing, Jackie grew tired of the daily struggles to find restaurants and hotels that would serve African Americans. He could not live with that kind of **discrimination**, and Jackie began to think about leaving baseball altogether.

Jackie played for the Kansas City Monarchs.

Little did Jackie know that someone was watching him play. That someone was Branch Rickey, the president of the Brooklyn Dodgers. He had wanted to break the color barrier in Major League baseball for some time but had never been successful.

The new head of Major League baseball was open to the idea. Still, Rickey was cautious. He did not go public with his plans to sign an African American player but instead pretended that he had plans to start a new African American team, to be called the Brooklyn Brown Dodgers.

Under this **guise**, he sent scouts around the country looking for talented African American players. In August of 1945, one of these scouts approached Jackie Robinson, inviting him to Brooklyn to meet with Branch Rickey.

Rickey knew that Jackie had both the talent and the strength to play in the Major Leagues. In their meeting,

Rickey told Jackie that he was not recruiting him for the Brooklyn *Brown* Dodgers. He wanted Jackie to play in the Majors, for the Brooklyn Dodgers, and he would start him with their farm team, the Montreal Royals. Even as Rickey described the horrible things players and fans might do or say, Jackie knew that he wanted to try. More than anything, he wanted to open the door for all players, regardless of color, to play Major League baseball.

Jackie signed a contract with the Montreal Royals, the farm team for the Brooklyn Dodgers.

Before he began his training with the Royals, Jackie took a few months off. During this time, Jackie and Rachel Isum were married, and the two of them traveled together to Florida when it was time for training camp to begin. Throughout Jackie's career in baseball, Rachel was a constant support.

The Major Leagues

Jackie's Montreal Royals teammates eventually warmed up to his presence. In some places, the team met record crowds and enthusiastic fans, but in others, Jackie faced terrible insults from both players and fans.

Even in the face of such **adversity**, Jackie played incredible baseball. The Montreal Royals won the Little World Series, thanks in good part to Jackie. That thrill was surpassed only by the birth of his first son, Jack Roosevelt Robinson, Jr., on November 18, 1946.

The following spring, just five days before the season opener, Branch Rickey announced that Jackie Robinson would be playing for the Brooklyn Dodgers. At first, there was serious opposition. Several of the Dodgers' players threatened to **strike**, while others asked to be traded. On other teams, players threatened to strike rather than play against an African American man. Finally, the president of the National League issued a statement saying that he did not care if half the league went on strike. Those who did would suffer the consequences. "This is the United States of America," he said, "and one citizen has as much right to play as another."

But playing was not easy. Opposing players and sometimes spectators in the stands hurled insults at Jackie. He knew that if he stood up for himself, if he started answering back, he might risk ruining everything. If a fight broke out, it would end the chance for other African Americans to play in the Majors. By standing firm and not **descending** to the level of his attackers, Jackie won the respect of his team and many fans across the country.

Despite protests, Jackie joined the Brooklyn Dodgers, breaking the "color barrier."

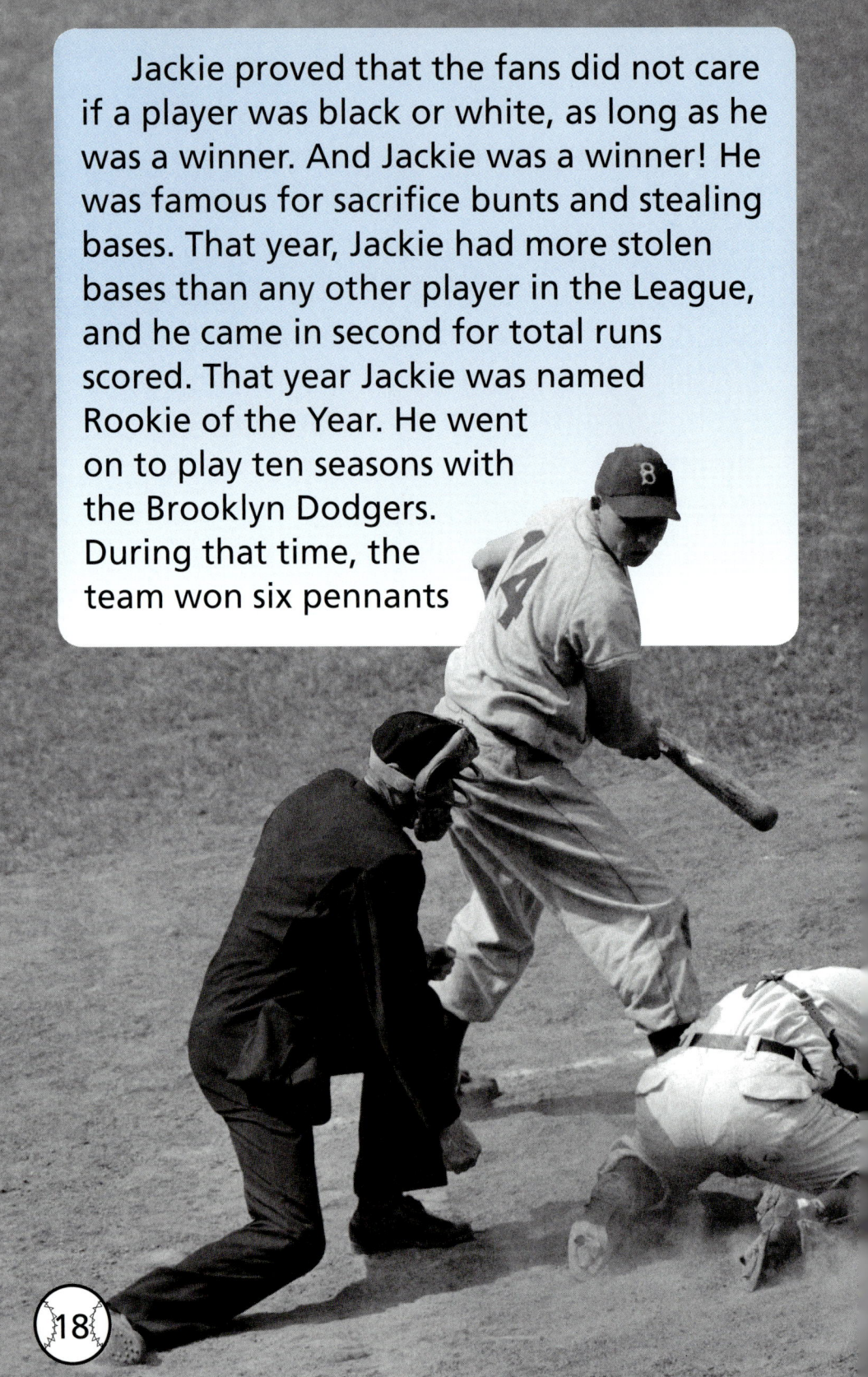

Jackie proved that the fans did not care if a player was black or white, as long as he was a winner. And Jackie was a winner! He was famous for sacrifice bunts and stealing bases. That year, Jackie had more stolen bases than any other player in the League, and he came in second for total runs scored. That year Jackie was named Rookie of the Year. He went on to play ten seasons with the Brooklyn Dodgers. During that time, the team won six pennants and beat the New York Yankees to win the World Series in 1955. Jackie also won the hearts of millions of fans.

Jackie's Legacy

Jackie's success paved the way for other African American players to join the Majors. One by one, other teams followed suit. By 1959, twelve years after Jackie Robinson broke the color barrier, every team in Major League baseball had at least one African American player. In 1962, Jackie Robinson was the first African American to be elected to the Baseball Hall of Fame. But Jackie's commitment to fighting for equality and civil rights did not end with the integration of baseball.

The fans turned out in record numbers to see Jackie and the Dodgers play. In this 1949 game, Jackie slid hard to steal home but was tagged out by Rube Walker of the Chicago Cubs.

Though he will always be remembered as the first African American to play in the Major Leagues, baseball was just one part of Jackie's **legacy**. Throughout his life, Jackie fought for civil rights, wanting to improve the lives of African Americans and others.

After he retired from baseball, Jackie and his wife, Rachel, participated in voter registration drives to register African American voters. They raised money to support Martin Luther King, Jr.'s, organization, the Southern Christian Leadership Conference (SCLC). Jackie spoke out against segregation and tried to get other athletes involved in the civil rights movement. He once said, "A life is not important except for the impact it has on other lives." Jackie's life was dedicated to service.

Jackie continued to work for civil rights for the rest of his life.

Late in his life, Jackie struggled with his health. Doctors diagnosed him with diabetes. By the time he was in his late forties, he had started to lose his sight. On October 24, 1972, Jackie suffered a heart attack and died. He was only fifty-three years old.

Jackie's life was an example of the importance of standing up for what you believe in. He never stopped working to help others. Even today, his strength and accomplishments are an inspiration to us all.

Now Try This

There were many other talented players in the Negro Leagues. Many of them never got a chance to play in the Majors. Others did and were even inducted into the Hall of Fame.

Here's How to Do It!

Find out more about some of these amazing players and the teams for which they played.
- Use a library or the Internet to find information.
- Write a brief report or a biography of a player.
- Share what you learn with a parent or friend.

From left: Jackie Robinson, George Crowe, Joe Black, Sam Jethroe, Roy Campanella, and Bill Bruton.

Hank Aaron

Willie Mays

Ernie Banks

23

Glossary

adversity *n.* hostile opposition or challenging circumstances

descending *v.* going down; lowering oneself

discrimination *n.* unfair treatment based on prejudice

guise *n.* a false appearance (as in disguise)

legacy *n.* the lasting contributions of a person or event

scholarships *n.* gifts of money or support to help a student in college or other studies

segregated *adj.* requiring separate areas or facilities for people of different races

sharecropper *n.* a farmer who does not own the land he lives or works on, but instead rents it from the owner and pays with a portion of the crops produced

strike *v.* to refuse to work as a way of protesting